# ACTION SCIENCE

# THE SCIENCE OF HITTING A HOME RUN

## FORCES AND MOTION IN ACTION

by Jim Whiting

Consultant:
Paul Ohmann, PhD
Associate Professor of Physics
University of St. Thomas, St. Paul, Minnesota

CAPSTONE PRESS
a capstone imprint

Fact Finders is published by Capstone Press,
1710 Roe Crest Drive, North Mankato, Minnesota 56003.
www.capstonepub.com

 Books published by Capstone Press are manufactured with paper
containing at least 10 percent post-consumer waste.

*Library of Congress Cataloging-in-Publication Data*
Whiting, Jim, 1943–
    The science of hitting a home run: forces and motion in action / by Jim Whiting.
    p. cm. — (Fact finders. Action science.)
    Summary: "Describes the science behind hitting a home run, including pitch types, different bats, and
force" — Provided by publisher.
    Includes bibliographical references and index.
    ISBN 978-1-4296-3953-8 (library binding)
    ISBN 978-1-4296-4854-7 (paperback)
    1. Baseball — Juvenile literature. 2. Force and energy — Juvenile literature. 3. Motion — Juvenile literature.
I. Title.
GV867.5.W45 2010
796.357'26 — dc22                                            2009033239

**Editorial Credits**
Lori Shores, editor; Lori Bye, designer; Jo Miller, media researcher; Eric Manske, production specialist

**Photo Credits:**
AP Images, 28 (bottom); David J. Phillip, cover
Getty Images Inc./Doug Pensinger, 25, 28 (top); Jim McIsaac, 12, 15; Jim Rogash, 9, 11; Lisa Blumenfeld, 26
Newscom, 17, 20
Shutterstock/Dennis Ku, 6–7 (all), 21; Kelpfish, 8, 13, 23; Ken Inness, 16, 19, 29; R. Gino Santa Maria, 5;
    scargut, 3 (design element); Todd Taulman, 22; TRINACRIA PHOTO, 18

The publisher does not endorse products whose logos may appear on objects in images in this book.

Essential content terms are **bold** and are defined at the bottom of the page where they first appear.

# TABLE OF CONTENTS

# THE FAN FAVORITE

For baseball fans, there's nothing better than a day at the ballpark. As you settle into your seat, the big scoreboard catches your eye. You scan the crowd and spot a vendor selling peanuts. The umpire shouts "Play ball!" and the first batter steps up to the plate.

But there's more action going on that you can't see. In a way, a ballpark is a big science lab. If you're really paying attention, you can spot some great science in action. Science rules everything that happens in the game, from a humming fastball to a home run.

From Little League to Major League, the home run is king. Nothing else brings baseball fans to their feet with more excitement. All eyes are on the ball rising far above the field. The crowd goes wild as the ball clears the fence. The fans may not know it, but science can explain exactly how a home run happens.

When baseball players take the field, science is there to pump up the action.

# CHAPTER 1

# THE PITCH

The batter holds his bat, ready for the pitch. He watches closely as the pitcher starts his windup. The pitcher raises his knee to his chest. With the ball in one hand, he raises his arms high. He reaches back, pushes off his back foot, and kicks forward. As his foot comes down, his arm moves up, over, and past his head. He shifts his weight forward and releases the ball.

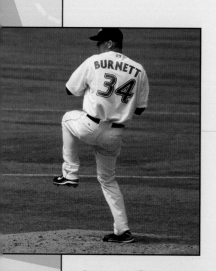

A pitcher's windup might look a little strange, but it creates a great deal of **momentum**. The full-body whipping motion is an example of a science concept called summation of movement. One body part moves first and transfers its energy to the next part. The pitcher transfers the momentum from his body to the ball, releasing it with great power and speed.

**momentum** — the motion carried by an object

The ball zips toward home plate at more than 90 miles (145 kilometers) per hour. The pitcher has thrown a fastball. A few major-league pitchers throw fastballs at 100 miles (161 kilometers) an hour or more. But a baseball traveling toward home plate loses speed because of **drag**. As the ball pushes through the air, the air pushes back, slowing the ball down. The disturbed airflow behind the ball, called the wake, causes drag too.

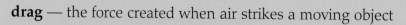

drag — the force created when air strikes a moving object

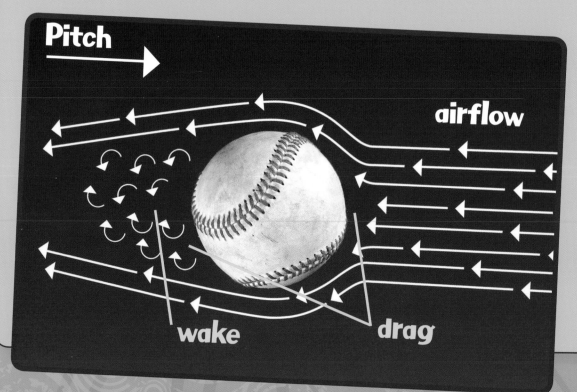

Pitch

airflow

wake

drag

## SEE FOR YOURSELF

To try out the pitcher's windup yourself, just grab a ball and head to the park. First stand still with your hips facing forward as you throw a baseball. Mark where the ball lands. Now try using a windup before throwing the ball. When you throw without moving your whole body, you only transfer the momentum of your arm and hand. Using the pitcher's windup builds up a lot of momentum. When you transfer that momentum to the ball, it flies farther.

The batter has less than a second to guess where and when the ball will cross home plate. He thinks it's a fastball, but he can't be sure.

Traveling at 90 miles (145 kilometers) per hour, the ball will reach home plate in about .45 second. At least .15 second is needed for the batter's brain to understand what he is seeing. If he decides to go for it, he'll need another .15 second to swing the bat. Just .15 second is left for the batter to make up his mind, barely the blink of an eye.

The batter needs lightning-fast **reflexes** to hit a home run. Years of practice have taught him to identify the pitch and swing at it, almost without thinking.

———◆———

**reflex** — an action that happens without a person's control or effort

The pitcher's mound is 60 feet, 6 inches (18.4 meters) from home plate.

Is it a fastball or a changeup? The batter isn't sure. A changeup looks like a fastball but isn't thrown as hard. The ball takes an extra .05 second to reach home plate. Often the batter is fooled by the pitch and swings too early. Pitchers also vary the path of their pitches to confuse batters. The way a pitcher grips the ball as he throws creates spin when the ball is released. Spin can make the ball curve, rise, or dip as it flies through the air.

If this pitch is a curveball, it will curve to one side and drop.

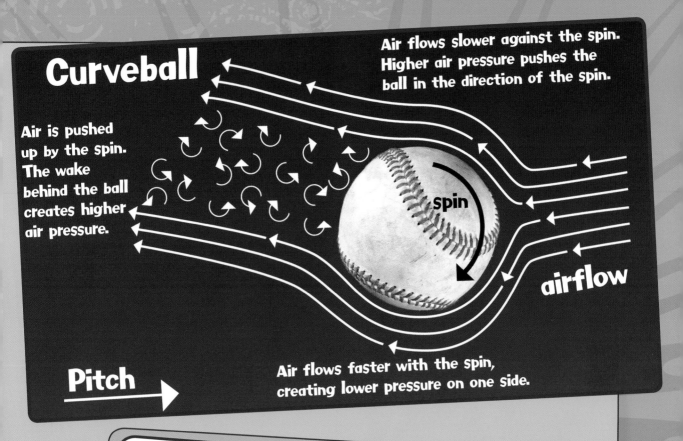

# Curveball

Air flows slower against the spin. Higher air pressure pushes the ball in the direction of the spin.

Air is pushed up by the spin. The wake behind the ball creates higher air pressure.

spin

airflow

Pitch →

Air flows faster with the spin, creating lower pressure on one side.

## The Sneaky Curveball

Curveballs spin sideways, making the air move faster on one side of the ball. The change in airflow makes the ball curve to one side and drop just before it reaches home plate. A left-handed pitcher's curveball curves away from a left-handed batter, making it hard to hit. In 2006, left-hander Jim Thome slammed a homer once every 8.2 times at bat facing right-handed pitchers. Against lefties, he managed a home run just once every 31.8 at bats.

13

# CHAPTER 2

# THE SWING

The batter has decided to swing. What happens next determines if he's going to slam a home run. The way his body moves as he swings is another example of summation of movement. This time the momentum is transferred from his body to the bat.

The batter holds the bat back behind his head with his hands just above the knob of the bat at chest level. He cocks his hips and takes a short step forward. His front hip swivels away from the plate as his rear hip moves forward.

He starts his swing, bringing the bat forward across home plate in an arc. The batter shifts his weight onto his front foot. His movements transfer momentum from his legs and arms to his hands and finally to the bat.

## SEE FOR YOURSELF

The size and weight of a ball affect how far it flies before drag slows it down. Try hitting a softball and a Wiffle ball to see which one flies the farthest. The softball has more surface area pushing through the air. The Wiffle ball has holes to let air pass through, creating less drag.

The batter uses the muscles of his legs, hips, and back to add power to his swing.

The bat is a blur of wood as it crosses home plate at 80 miles (129 kilometers) per hour. Many major-league players use bats that weigh 32 ounces (.9 kilograms). Baseball players spend years figuring out the best weight to use. Heavy bats transfer more **kinetic energy** to the ball than light bats. But heavy bats as aren't easy to swing. Lighter bats are easier to control and can be swung faster. A hit baseball will travel 8 feet (2.4 meters) farther for every 1 mile (1.6 kilometers) per hour a batter can add to his swing.

———•———

**kinetic energy** — the energy of a moving object

Most hitters wear batting gloves to improve their grip on the bat.

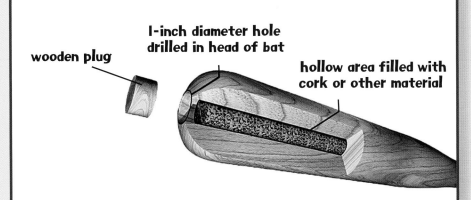

## Corking a Baseball Bat

wooden plug

1-inch diameter hole drilled in head of bat

hollow area filled with cork or other material

## Corking a Bat

Some baseball players drill holes in their bats and fill them with cork to make them lighter. In 2003, Chicago Cubs slugger Sammy Sosa was caught using a corked bat. These bats are against Major League Baseball rules. But if Sosa had known the science involved, he might not have risked the penalty. When a corked bat strikes a ball, the soft cork takes in some of the kinetic energy. Less energy is left for the ball, which then travels slower.

The batter keeps his eye on the ball. He knows a home run takes more than just a fast swing. To hit a long ball, the ball must strike the bat's sweet spot. This area is about 5 to 7 inches (13 to 18 centimeters) from the fat end of the bat. Hitting the ball outside this area sets off **vibrations** in the wood. Vibrations waste energy that could have been passed on to the ball. As a result, some of the swing's power is lost. But hitting the ball at the sweet spot doesn't cause vibrations. At the sweet spot, the ball receives the most energy and flies the farthest.

**vibration** — a fast movement back and forth

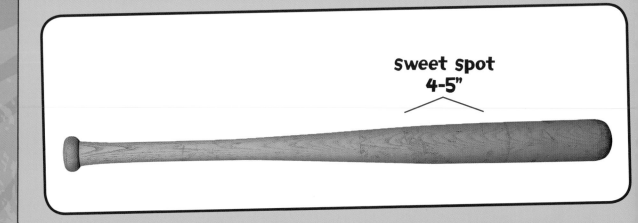

sweet spot
4-5"

Vibrations in the bat can also hurt the batter's hands.

## SEE FOR YOURSELF

To find a bat's sweet spot, curl your fingers around the knob at the end. Then let the bat dangle. Have a friend tap the barrel of the bat with a hammer. You'll feel the vibrations. Have your friend continue tapping, moving the hammer along the bat. When the vibrations stop, mark that spot with a piece of tape. Continue tapping, and put another piece of tape where the vibrations start again. The area between the two pieces of tape is the sweet spot.

# CHAPTER 3

# THE HIT

Crack! The ball smashes into the bat. The ball is traveling about 90 miles (145 kilometers) per hour. The bat is moving at about 80 miles (129 kilometers) per hour. That's a combined impact of 170 miles (274 kilometers) per hour. Two cars crashing at those speeds would become twisted masses of mangled metal. But a baseball is different. The yarn-covered cork and rubber center of the baseball takes in part of the energy of the hit.

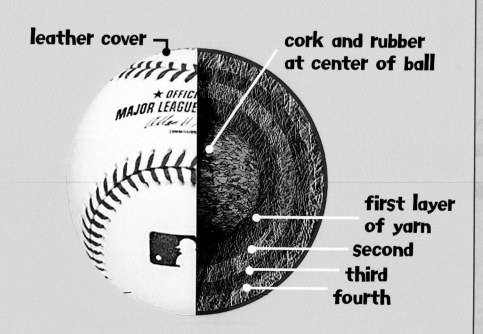

leather cover

cork and rubber at center of ball

first layer of yarn

second

third

fourth

Players who hit a lot of home runs are called "power hitters."

For a split second, the ball stops. The force of the impact squishes the ball to about half its original size. But the ball uses the energy from the hit to bounce back to its original shape. The ball has used some of the energy of the hit. But it still rockets off the bat at around 110 miles (177 kilometers) per hour.

A good hitter follows through with the swing to create the most speed and power.

The hitter drops the bat as he takes off toward first base. Fans hold their breath as the ball rises into the air. Thanks to the batter's slight upward swing, the ball is spinning in the opposite direction in which it is flying. Backspin happens when the air pressure is greater on the bottom of the ball than on the top. The bottom air pressure produces **lift** to keep the ball flying through the air longer.

Backspin also helps to cancel out some of the effects of drag. With backspin, the ball cuts through the air more easily. Topspin, on the other hand, makes the ball come down sooner. A ball with topspin spins in the same direction as its flight.

———●———

**lift** — an upward force

# Backspin
## path of ball →

**Air flows faster in the direction of the spin, creating lower air pressure above the ball.**

**Air pushed down by the spin adds to high air pressure under the ball, creating lift.**

**Air flows slower against the spin, creating more air pressure under the ball.**

23

# CHAPTER 4

# HEAT, HEIGHT, AND HOME RUNS

Anything can happen in a baseball game. And some things are out of the players' control. Say the wind is blowing toward home plate. A hit ball that might have been a home run could be held back and caught. When the wind blows away from home plate, the moving air pushes the ball farther. A ball that might have been caught has a chance to clear the fence.

Hitters love hot weather. Because hot air expands, or gets bigger, less air moves on the surface of the ball. Less air pressure creates less drag, so the ball can fly farther. Hot weather has another benefit. Hot air is thinner than cool air. Curveballs don't curve as well in thin air. Instead, they become "hanging curveballs" that stay out over the plate and often turn into home runs.

Baseballs hit at Coors Field will fly 10 percent farther than those hit at sea level.

Hitters also love Coors Field in Denver, Colorado. This stadium sits more than 5,000 feet (1,524 meters) above sea level. The higher you go, the thinner the air gets. A baseball flies easily through thinner air because there is less drag. A ball that would be caught at sea level might soar another 20 feet (6 meters) at Coors Field.

Will the ball clear the fence? Will it fly, fly, fly away, as some baseball announcers say? Will it be going, going, gone?

Your eyes are glued to the ball as it sails over the fence. You hear the announcer shout, "It's outta here!" It's a home run! You jump up, glove in hand, just in time to nab the ball.

It's one of more than 5,000 home runs hit every year in major league baseball. But that doesn't make it less amazing. The crowd goes wild. The batter can hear the fans chanting his name from the stands. But they really should chant "SCI-ENCE! SCI-ENCE! SCI-ENCE!" After all, it's science that made the home run possible.

## BATTER FACTS

• Barry Bonds holds the records for home runs in a single season (73) and lifetime (762). Many fans believe that he used drugs called steroids to reach those records. Steroids build bigger muscles, which help hitters swing harder. But these drugs are also against the rules.

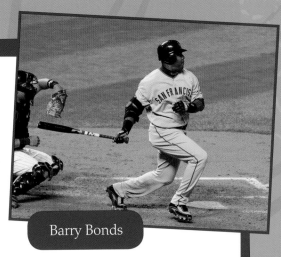

Barry Bonds

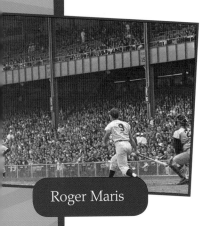

Roger Maris

• Roger Maris hit 61 home runs in 1961 to break Babe Ruth's record of 60. As he neared Ruth's record, Maris' hair started falling out due to stress. High levels of stress use up the body's energy. There isn't much energy left over to grow nails and hair.

• On April 17, 1953, New York Yankee Mickey Mantle hit the longest official home run in baseball history. The ball traveled 565 feet (172 meters). That day, there was a strong wind blowing from home plate toward the outfield.

# OTHER SCIENCES IN ACTION

**Radar Technology** — A radar gun behind home plate measures pitch speed. The gun shoots electromagnetic waves at the baseball. These waves are a special form of light. They are like the waves used by cell phones and radios. The waves strike the ball and return to the gun. Changes in the waves show how fast the ball was moving.

**Medical Science** — In 1974, pitcher Tommy John tore a ligament in his arm. Surgeon Frank Jobe cut a tendon from John's other arm and used it to replace the torn ligament. John pitched for 14 more years. Today the operation is common. Nearly 10 percent of major-league pitchers have had Tommy John surgery.

**Botany** — Most major-league players use bats made of maple or ash wood. Maple bats are harder and last longer, but they can break without warning. Cracks appear in ash bats when they wear out, so they can be replaced before they shatter.

# Glossary

**botany** (BAH-tuh-nee) — the scientific study of plants

**concept** (KON-sept) — a general idea or understanding of something

**drag** (DRAG) — the force created when air strikes a moving object; drag slows down moving objects.

**kinetic energy** (ki-NET-ik EN-ur-jee) — the energy of a moving object

**lift** (LIFT) — an upward force

**ligament** (LIG-uh-muhnt) — a band of tissue that connects bones

**momentum** (moh-MEN-tuhm) — the motion carried by an object

**reflex** (REE-fleks) — an action that happens without a person's control or effort

**steroid** (STER-oid) — an illegal drug that can increase a person's strength and athletic ability; steroids can cause heart problems and death.

**tendon** (TEN-duhn) — a band of tissue that connects a muscle to a bone

**vibration** (vye-BRAY-shuhn) — a fast movement back and forth

# Read More

**Bonnet, Robert L., and Dan Keen.** *Home Run! Science Projects With Baseball and Softball.* Score! Sports Science Projects. Berkeley Heights, N.J.: Enslow, 2009.

**Bow, James.** *Baseball Science.* Sports Science. New York: Crabtree, 2009.

**Thomas, Keltie.** *How Baseball Works.* How Sports Work. Berkeley, Calif.: Maple Tree Press, 2008.

# Internet Sites

FactHound offers a safe, fun way to find Internet sites related to this book. All of the sites on FactHound have been researched by our staff.

Here's all you do:

Visit *www.facthound.com*

FactHound will fetch the best sites for you!

# Index